IMAGES OF WAR

GERMAN ASSAULT GUNS
AND
TANK DESTROYERS
1940–1945

The front of this German Marder III Ausf M took a direct hit in Normandy in 1944, shattering the front plate armour. The left-hand drive sprocket and road wheels have been torn off.

IMAGES OF WAR

GERMAN ASSAULT GUNS
AND
TANK DESTROYERS
1940–1945

RARE PHOTOGRAPHS FROM
WARTIME ARCHIVES

Anthony Tucker-Jones

Pen & Sword
MILITARY

First published in Great Britain in 2016 by
PEN & SWORD MILITARY
an imprint of
Pen & Sword Books Ltd,
47 Church Street,
Barnsley,
South Yorkshire
S70 2AS

A CIP record for this book is available from the British Library.

ISBN 978 147384 599 2

Typeset by CHIC GRAPHICS

Printed and bound by CPI Group (UK) Ltd, Croydon, CR0 4YY

Pen & Sword Books Ltd incorporates the imprints of Pen & Sword Archaeology,
Atlas, Aviation, Battleground, Discovery, Family History, History, Maritime, Military,
Naval, Politics, Railways, Select, Social History, Transport, True Crime, Claymore
Press, Frontline Books, Leo Cooper, Praetorian Press, Remember When, Seaforth
Publishing and Wharncliffe.

For a complete list of Pen & Sword titles please contact
Pen & Sword Books Limited
47 Church Street, Barnsley, South Yorkshire, S70 2AS, England
E-mail: enquiries@pen-and-sword.co.uk
Website: www.pen-and-sword.co.uk

Contents

Introduction:
An Independent Weapon

This photographic history visually chronicles the hugely successful range of German assault guns, tank destroyers and tank hunters which were developed during the Second World War. As the conflict progressed, the German Army had to find a use for its obsolete panzers and this gave rise to vehicles such as the turretless Sturmgeschütz, designed for an infantry support role. From 1943 Hitler's assault guns and tank destroyers played a vital role in Nazi Germany's increasingly defensive war.

One of the great advantages of the Sturmgeschütz was its low profile. General Hasso von Manteuffel, summing up Hitler's Panzerwaffe (armoured force), said: 'Fire-power, armour protection, speed and cross-country performance are the essentials, and the best type of tank is that which combines these conflicting requirements with most success. In my opinion the German Panzer V, the Panther, was the most satisfactory of all, and would have been close to ideal had it been possible to design it with a lower silhouette.'

Lacking turrets, the German assault guns, tank destroyers and tank hunters were primarily designed to support the infantry and panzergrenadier divisions, and were a very distinct fighting arm from the Panzerwaffe. Because the assault guns equipped the assault artillery batteries, they came under the direct command of the German Army's artillery and not the Panzerwaffe, which resulted in a needless turf war.

As the conflict progressed, these armoured vehicles deployed with the independent StuG brigades, the assault gun detachments, Panzerjäger detachments and tank detachments of infantry and panzer divisions. Often a lack of tanks meant that they were called on to fill the panzers' role. They proved ideal during the massive defensive battles fought on the Eastern Front, as well as in Italy and Normandy, and ultimately they were instrumental in delaying the defeat of Hitler's Nazi Germany.

German self-propelled guns operated in a variety of roles but with the focus on serving as a platform for anti-tank guns or field artillery. It is important to clarify that German self-propelled guns consisted of both open-topped and enclosed fighting compartments installed on a vast variety of tank chassis. These were termed

Panzerjäger (tank hunter) or Sturmgeschütz (assault gun), utilising light and medium tank chassis respectively. Confusingly, the latter were initially organised into battalions and then brigades were renamed Sturmartillerie (assault artillery). The Germans also used the term Jagdpanzer (hunting tank); these were essentially more heavily armoured versions of the Panzerjäger, using medium and heavy tank chassis. In Western parlance, both types were simply considered tank destroyers.

Although the primary role of the assault gun evolved from assault artillery to anti-tank weapon, these units came under the responsibility of the artillery. This meant that the StuG crews were gunners and not panzertruppen. The backbone of such units were the various model StuG III, StuG IV and StuH42 fully enclosed assault guns. In contrast, the Panzerjäger and Jagdpanzer, which were dedicated tank killers, were largely manned by the panzer arm.

Although the assault gun units occasionally served within the panzer and panzergrenadier divisions, they were usually controlled at either Corps or Army level and were allocated on a temporary basis to units that needed their firepower. In the second half of the war assault guns also served as dedicated units within the infantry, panzergrenadier and panzer divisions.

Equally confusingly for the uninitiated, while the bulk of the lighter Panzerjäger armoured vehicles were open-topped, they later included enclosed heavier hunting tanks such as the Jagdpanzer, Jagdpanther* and Jagdtiger.** Initially the hastily designed Panzerjäger were formed as a stopgap using a variety of German or captured Czech and French light tank chassis armed with Czech, French and Russian guns. The most noteworthy were a series of Czech-based vehicles known as the Marder, and the purpose-built heavy tank destroyers such as the Nashhorn, based on the Panzer Mk IV,*** and the Jagdpanther, utilising the Panther tank.

Panzerjäger were distributed liberally and from 1941 onwards were issued to the integral anti-tank battalions of the infantry, panzer and panzergrenadier divisions, as well as to the anti-tank companies of infantry and panzergrenadier regiments and to independent Army and Corps units. Although the field artillery regiments of the panzer and panzergrenadier divisions started the war with towed guns, during the period 1942–45 self-propelled artillery mountings, such as the Hummel and the Wespe, became available.

Unfortunately for General Heinz Guderian, in his role as overseer of Hitler's Panzerwaffe, he soon fell victim to inter-service rivalry, which was to greatly and needlessly hamper vital tank production. His level of authority and direct access to

---

* For more information see Anthony Tucker-Jones, *The Panther Tank. Hitler's T-34 Killer* (Pen & Sword, 2016)
** For more information see Anthony Tucker-Jones, *Tiger I and Tiger II* (Pen & Sword, 2014)
*** For more information see Anthony Tucker-Jones, *The Panzer IV: Hitler's Rock* (Pen & Sword, forthcoming, 2017)

the Führer caused deep resentment within certain elements of the German High Command, who sought to avoid his authority. Guderian's terms of reference, signed by Hitler on 28 February 1943, stated:

> The Inspector-General of Armoured Troops is responsible to me for the future development of armoured troops along lines that will make that arm of Service into a decisive weapon for winning the war.
>
> The Inspector-General of Armoured Troops is directly subordinate to myself. He has the command powers of an army commander and is the senior officer of armoured troops.

The term 'armoured troops' was all-encompassing and included tank troops, panzergrenadiers, motorised infantry, armoured reconnaissance troops, anti-tank troops and heavy assault units. Guderian had deliberately included the artillery's assault guns because they were taking up such a high proportion of tank production. In Guderian's view, the calibre of the guns on these vehicles and the towed anti-tank guns was insufficient. He wanted to provide the infantry divisions with assault guns, in place of the towed guns, and to provide the panzer divisions with assault guns only until tank production was sufficient to meet their requirements. In some quarters this was seen as heresy.

However, the word 'heavy' was inserted into his terms of reference regarding the assault guns, which meant Guderian only had authority over the latest heavy Jagdtiger and Jagdpanther, while the thousands of medium Sturmgeschütz remained beyond his jurisdiction. During his first conference with Hitler on 9 March 1943 he tried to rectify the situation, but the assembled staff refused to relinquish command of the assault guns and Hitler would not extend Guderian's authority.

Guderian recalled, with some bitterness: 'The results of this decision were far-reaching: the assault artillery remained an independent weapon; the anti-tank battalions continued to be equipped with ineffective, tractor-drawn guns, and the infantry divisions remained without adequate anti-tank defence.' It was not until the end of 1943 that Guderian finally got his way and his authority was extended, by which time it was too late.

The attitude of the artillery commanders is perhaps understandable as they were regarded as the poorer cousins by the rest of the German Army. Throughout the 1930s the artillery had seen its authority eroded; as it was developed, anti-tank artillery came under the panzer arm, the Luftwaffe took over anti-aircraft artillery and the Kriegsmarine took control of coastal artillery. This meant that the Panzerwaffe and the Luftwaffe supplied much of the close fire support for the infantry during mobile operations, as the artillery was unequipped for such a role.

At the outbreak of the war the bulk of the German artillery consisted of 105mm and 150mm guns, most of which was horse-drawn rather than motorised.

The artillery units, with their red piping insignia, kept control of, and manned, most of the medium assault guns because they had powerful supporters in the senior circles of the German Army. Both the army commanders-in-chief were career artillerymen, along with the first two chiefs of the army general staff; those field commanders of high rank who were first commissioned in the artillery included von Leeb, von Kluge, von Küchler and von Reichenau.

Guderian was acutely aware that the infantry's 37mm, 50mm and 75mm towed anti-tank guns were simply not mobile enough, nor did they offer sufficient protection to the crews, especially when engaging enemy tanks. He recognised that something had to be done about this situation – but Hitler simply would not listen. Guderian's attempts to centralise the development of armoured warfare at a crucial moment in the war failed.

At the very start of the Second World War the assault artillery was intended to provide close fire support for the advancing infantry by blasting enemy bunkers and weapons positions. Once the tide of the conflict began to turn against Nazi Germany, tank hunters began to play an increasingly important role in strengthening the panzers in the tank-on-tank battles. By 1942 self-propelled guns were increasingly coming into their own as they were used to stop enemy tanks. This was in part because removing the restricted space of a tank turret enabled the large fixed superstructure to take larger calibre and longer-range guns.

Once Hitler's Wehrmacht was consigned to fighting a largely defensive war on both the Eastern and Western Fronts, the lack of all-round gun traverse was not a major problem: when an assault gun was dug in, it presented an even smaller target than its counterparts, becoming a deadly defensive weapon. The reality was that German assault and self-propelled guns actually eclipsed the panzers. They were cheaper and quicker to build and by the end of the war had often supplanted the tank within the panzer battalions.

Limited numbers of assault guns participated in the 1940 Blitzkrieg in Western Europe. Likewise, very small numbers of assault guns and tank destroyers saw combat in the campaigns in North Africa. These were not sufficient to have any real bearing on the conflict. In Italy assault guns and tank destroyers, not panzers, were ideally suited to Hitler's defensive war and he even pressed into service captured Italian Semovente assault guns. In France in 1944 the StuG, fighting alongside the panzers, excelled as an ambush weapon in the confines of the Normandy hedgerows and played a key part in holding up the Allies for three long months.

It was on the Eastern Front in the summer of 1944 that Hitler's enthusiasm for the StuG backfired. Army Group Centre found itself bereft of panzers and completely reliant on StuG and Panzerjäger units. These proved completely incapable of stopping the Red Army and when the panzers did arrive it was too late to prevent the wholesale collapse of Army Group Centre. This left the Red Army at the very gates of Warsaw and spelt the end of Nazi Germany.

General Heinz Guderian, one of the key architects of Hitler's panzer forces in the 1930s, was not a big fan of the assault gun concept. He saw it for what it was: an infantry support weapon ideal for defence but not offence. The StuG and Jagdpanzer, he reasoned, lacked the flexibility of the panzer capable of firing in all directions. Guderian was extremely unhappy that the Panzer IV medium tank, which provided the backbone of the Panzerwaffe throughout the war, was dissipated by StuG IV and Jagdpanzer IV production. Indeed, the numerous variants of StuG and Panzerjäger were symptomatic of the German inability to come up with a single utilitarian design and stick with it.

The StuG and Jagdpanzer also showed that by the end of the war the German armoured doctrine had come full circle, from offence to defence. Guderian and his colleagues may have argued that attack was the best form of defence, but this was not what Hitler's assault guns and tank destroyers were designed for. They remained an independent defensive weapon.

Photograph Sources

The images in this book have been sourced via the author from various archives including the US Army and US Signal Corps, as well as his own considerable collection.

Chapter One

Sturmgeschütz III
Ausf A, B, C/D and E

At the same time that Hitler was developing his panzers, a requirement for a German infantry support armoured fighting vehicle was issued on 15 June 1936. This was to be dubbed the Sturmgeschütz (assault gun). The concept was sound and logical in that it would provide artillery and anti-tank gun crews with a level of armoured protection from indirect and direct fire while fighting toe-to-toe with the enemy. The intention was to develop a limited profile armoured vehicle that was no higher than the average soldier. To facilitate this meant the vehicle would have to be turretless, resulting in the gun being mounted in the hull with a minimum of 25 degrees traverse.

Five experimental 0-serie (series) Sturmgeschütz were built on the chassis of Panzer III Ausf B (which had been first manufactured in 1937 and armed with a 37mm gun); they consisted of a soft steel superstructure containing a fixed short-barrelled 75mm StuK37 L/24 close support gun. These prototypes proved satisfactory and in January 1940 the 1 Serie Ausf A went into production.

Notably, the StuK37 (Sturmkanone) was mounted slightly offset to the right of the superstructure, providing more space for the driver seated to the left of the gun. The traverse was evenly divided with 12 degrees both left and right. The gun was primarily designed to fire high explosive rounds, and due to its low muzzle velocity it had poor armour-piercing capability against anything other than light tanks. Its maximum penetration was about 40mm of armour. This would not be remedied until the introduction of the vastly superior 75mm StuK40 L/43 and L/48 weapons on the StuG F and G models, which could cut through about 100m of armour.

The driver was provided with a pivoting visor on the front driver port, a vision port on the left of the superstructure, and a twin periscope in the superstructure front. The commander was provided with a scissor periscope that was raised after opening the front half of his access hatch. The gunner had a periscope sight in the upper left of the superstructure. The vehicle was capable of carrying forty-four rounds of ammunition, which were fed to the gun by the loader (the fourth member of the crew).

The StuG Ausf A lacked a machine gun for close protection, a defect that was not remedied until the StuG Ausf F. While it utilised the same suspension, drive train and basic hull shape as the Panzer III Ausf F, the front and rear of the StuG III Ausf A had thicker armour. Other changes included the brake access hatches on the glacis plate being hinged at the sides and not fore and aft, while the escape hatches on the hull sides were dispensed with. Extra armour could be added by attaching 9mm plates at an angle to the superstructure sides.

At 19.6 tons the Ausf A weighed almost as much as the Panzer III. Likewise, its length (5.38m) and width (2.92m) were largely comparable, although its height was only 1.95m compared to the 2.5m of the Panzer III. (The Panzer IV was almost 2.7m high and the Tiger and Panther almost 3m.) The StuG Ausf A was powered by a Maybach HL 120TR engine, with the gearbox providing ten forward and four reverse gears. Only thirty Ausf A were built by Alkett; they saw action in France in May 1940 with Sturmartillerie Batteries 640, 659, 660 and 665.

The follow-on B model saw 320 produced, seeing action in the Balkan and Russian campaigns of 1941. This model went into production in June 1941, and the only real differences from the Ausf A involved improvements to the drive train. The gears were reduced to six forward and one reverse. The only visual difference was that some of the later Ausf B were fitted with a new six-spoke drive sprocket and an eight-spoke idler designed for the wider 40cm track. Confusingly, the Ausf B was the 2nd and 3rd series of the StuG.

There were seven Sturmartillerie batteries by the end of 1940, as well as four assault artillery detachments, each with three batteries. Two Sturmartillerie battalions were involved in the invasion of the Balkans, and six were involved in the assault on the Soviet Union. A total of 105 assault guns were lost during these operations.

Some 200 Ausf C/D were produced as combat replacements in 1941, with just three Ausf D seeing action with the Afrika Korps the following year. These two models made up the 4th and 5th series of the StuG and featured an improved superstructure. The main changes were the removal of the direct vision port for the gunner's sight and the redesigning of the roof hatch above the gunner to permit the gunsight to be raised next to the closed hatch. Just fifty Ausf C were built and 150 Ausf D from May to September 1941. Some of the Ausf D were produced as commander's vehicles with the addition of an armoured pannier on the right side of the superstructure, similar to the left-hand one on all the Ausf A–D.

Some 200 Ausf E were built between September 1941 and March 1942. The original intention was to build 500 but the plan was abandoned after the long-barrelled 75mm StuK40 came into service. One Ausf E was used to trial the new gun while a second was used to trial the StuH assault howitzer concept. Another twelve Ausf E chassis were used for the StuIG33B assault infantry gun. The main visual difference on the E model was the addition of an armoured pannier on the right-hand side, and both left and right panniers were longer than those on the previous models. Also the glacis hatches were fitted with small hinges, doing away with the bulky ones employed on the previous versions.

The slanted 9mm armour plates on the sides of the superstructure were discontinued. A half-hearted attempt was made to provide some close protection against enemy infantry and aircraft in the form of an internally stowed MG34 machine gun. However, the StuG was not fitted with a gun mount or gun shield for the weapon, which meant that in using it a crewmember had to open the hatch and be exposed to enemy fire.

Most of the StuG Ausf E were used as combat loss replacements for existing units, but some went to new detachments. It is evident that the StuGs were in the thick of the fighting. By early July 1942 a total of 619 StuGs of all types were listed as combat ready; by July 1943 there were 142, of which just thirty-seven were deployed at the front.

The Ausf B was armed with the short-barrelled StuK37 L/24 75mm gun, similar to that installed on the Panzer IV, and more than 300 of these assault guns were produced from June 1940 to May 1941. This example is thought to have been photographed in Greece in 1941. It bears the unit number 331 and has a swastika flag draped over its nose plate for aerial recognition purposes.

A StuG III Ausf B assault gun in action. Note the spent shell cases, discarded by the gunner, by the road wheels. The Ausf A and Ausf B saw combat in France in 1940 and the Balkans in 1941, respectively.

Ausf B photographed during the invasion of the Soviet Union in the summer of 1941. Six Sturmartillerie battalions or assault artillery units took part in Hitler's massive Operation Barbarossa.

Another Ausf B photographed in the Soviet Union. The Ausf B was intended for infantry support and its main armament was designed primarily for firing high explosive, not armour-piercing, shells.

This preserved example of an early model Sturmgeschütz III Ausf B gives a good impression of the general concept behind the infantry support assault gun. Its low profile and larger calibre gun gave it some advantage over the Panzer III from which it was derived. However, its armour-piercing performance was poor due to low muzzle velocity.

Pressed into service by the Red Army, a captured Panzer III leads a column of four StuG III in March 1942. The Sturmgeschütz impressed the Soviets and as the war progressed they sought to emulate it with their own designs, most notably the SU-85 and SU-100 derived from the T-34 tank.

Opposite bottom left, above and below:
Ausf B or D in action on the Eastern Front. Some 200 Ausf C/D were built during the summer of 1941 as combat replacements for lost Ausf B.

A heavily damaged Ausf D belonging to *Sturmartillerie* Battalion 192. It has lost its drive sprocket and three road wheels – possibly as a result of running over an anti-tank mine on the Eastern Front in 1941.

In North Africa Erwin Rommel received very few dedicated assault guns such as this Sturmgeschütz Ausf D, having to rely instead on a hotchpotch of hybrid self-propelled guns mounted on captured Czech and French chassis. Sonderverband (Detachment for Special Employment) 288 took just three Ausf D to Africa in early 1942, seeing action at Gazala and Tobruk.

No doubt set up for the cameras, this shot shows an Ausf E finishing off a smoking Soviet T-34/76 tank at close range. The T-34 has lost a wheel and its tracks so the Sturmartillerie crew may be using it for target practice. It was intended to build 500 Ausf E but only 200 were completed.

Soviet troops with a captured StuG III Ausf E (distinguishable from earlier models by the square armoured side panniers). Production of this model stopped in March 1942 in favour of the upgunned Ausf F. Such redeployment by the Red Army was restricted by the availability of spares and ammunition.

An early model StuG taking on ammunition from a munitions carrier. Note the Sturmartillerie-style field jacket; their uniforms were essentially the same as those worn by the panzertruppen, but in field grey.

A Sturmartillerie crewman is decorated for bravery. This StuG III Ausf G crew are wearing the distinctive field-grey assault gun crew uniform; they were not technically permitted to wear black.

Chapter Two

Sturmgeschütz III
Ausf F and F/8

Following Hitler's invasion of the Soviet Union, it rapidly became apparent that the Red Army was deploying newer and superior tank types to those in its existing inventory. Specifically, the appearance of the Soviet KV-1 heavy tank and the T-34 medium tank was a worrying development that did not bode well for the Germans. During the summer of 1941 the Red Army had insufficient numbers of these and those that it did have suffered as a result of poor training. By the winter Soviet crews had realised that the T-34 had the makings of a first-class tank and its performance began to improve.

In response, Oberkommando der Wehrmacht (German Armed Forces High Command) issued instructions that Hitler wanted the StuG to be up-armoured and upgunned with the long-barrelled StuK40 75mm gun as soon as possible. At the same time the Panzer IV, armed with the short KwK37 75mm gun, was re-armed with the much more powerful long KwK40. This seemed to offer the best quick fix. The StuG Ausf F constituted the 6th in series from March to July 1942 and the 7th from July to September 1942.

There was little to distinguish the Ausf F's superstructure from that of the previous models except for the addition of a prominent circular exhaust fan to the right of the commander's hatch on the roof to remove gun fumes. Although the StuK40 gun was installed in the same place as the StuK37, it had a completely new bolted box-like gun mantlet that was vertical rather than horizontal and tapered in towards the gun. This was needed to contain the larger recoil of the much bigger gun. It also meant that the upper front of the superstructure was slightly enlarged to accommodate the mantlet and improve crew protection; this gave it a height of 2.15m, compared to the previous 1.98m. Some of the early models lacked muzzle brakes.

Most Ausf F were armed with the StuK40 L/43 but thirty-one were fitted with the later, slightly more powerful, L/48 gun. Both provided front-line troops with a much-needed antidote to the KV-1 and T-34. This weapon upgrade meant that the StuG Ausf F evolved from the artillery support role to a predominantly anti-tank role. Some Ausf F were fitted with additional armour (Zusatz Panzerung) from June 1942. Inevitably this led to a slight increase in weight from around 20 tons to 21.6 tons, resulting in a slight reduction in range from 160km to 140km. From a total of 359 Ausf F built, 182 had the additional armour.

The follow-on F/8 appeared in September 1942 and production ran until December that year. The main change with this model was the introduction of an improved hull design that drew on the Panzer III Ausf J and L. At the front the side plates extended beyond the front plate and had holes drilled to create towing brackets. The superstructure and the front of the hull were up-armoured with an additional 30mm of bolted-on armour. In addition, the thickness of the rear hull armour was boosted from 30mm to 50mm. The rear deck was extended further back and the air louvres were changed to increase engine ventilation.

In light of the inadequate gun in the Panzer III (which had been progressively upgraded from a 37mm to a 50mm and finally to the short 75mm), in 1942 Alkett was ordered to cease production of this tank and build only StuGs. As a gun tank the Panzer III would continue to be built until the summer of 1943 by Hitler's other panzer manufacturers. Alkett used a number of existing Mk III hulls for assault gun production and these could be identified by a distinctive single-piece forward-opening hatch over the final drive. Some 334 Ausf F/8 were built; four were converted to StuH42 and another twelve chassis were used for the StuIG33B.

Although the number of assault gun units continued to increase, the F/8 was largely issued as a combat replacement for battle-damaged Ausf E and Ausf F. In addition, some of the Waffen-SS panzer divisions received a Sturmgeschütz detachment equipped with Ausf F and Ausf F/8 in 1942.

The StuG III Ausf F was upgunned from earlier models by utilising the much more powerful long-barrelled 75mm StuK40 L/43 or L/48 gun. The bigger weapon required a much larger bolted box mantlet fitted above the barrel. Known as the F/8, this model deployed with Sturmgeschütz Brigade 303 in Finland in 1944. It is identifiable by the front towing brackets drilled through the extended side plates.

Opposite: This column of Ausf F, photographed on the Eastern Front with Sturmgeschütz Brigade 210, highlights the lack of a protective cupola for the commander, which inevitably left him exposed to enemy fire when emerging from the hatch. This problem was remedied with the Ausf G. Note the commander's and gunner's periscopes.

German infantry hitch a lift on three supporting Ausf F. On this version the front towing brackets were attached to the glacis plate and not the side plates, as with the F/8. Note the circular exhaust fan vent located just behind the soldier sitting on the gun mantlet.

Another Ausf F supporting advancing German infantry. This variant retained the long rectangular side panniers designed for the Ausf E.

This Ausf F has been camouflaged to blend in with the landscape. It belonged to the Sturmgeschütz detachment of the Luftwaffe's Herman Göring Division, which fought in Sicily, Italy and on the Eastern Front.

American troops marching past a knocked-out Ausf F or Ausf G at Santa Agata, northern Sicily, in 1943, following the landings of Operation Husky.

A very well known shot of an F/8 photographed on the streets of Athens. It very clearly shows attempts to up-armour the StuG with the addition of supplementary armour. This comprised 30mm armour plates bolted to the upper and lower nose plates, plus additional 20mm armour attached to the vertical plate. Perhaps not surprisingly, the bolt heads are very prominent.

This StuG III from Sturmgeschütz Brigade 907 was destroyed in Italy in 1944. The top of its superstructure has been blown clean off. It is either an F/8 or early model Ausf G; the angled side panniers indicate it is the latter.

British troops examining the damage to the nose plate armour on an Ausf G in Italy. The gun mantlet has been severely damaged, and to the left the bolt heads seem to have sheared off the additional vertical armour plate. Judging by the rings on the gun barrel, this StuG claimed five enemy tanks before it was knocked out.

Soviet troops wander past an Ausf G destroyed during the liberation of Sevastopol in 1944. StuGs saw extensive combat in the Crimea. This vehicle is missing its roof.

StuG III serving with the Finnish Army captured by the Red Army. The apparent lack of a commander's cupola suggests that it is an Ausf F, but the superstructure is that of an Ausf G.

The crew of an Ausf F take a break from the fighting. This example has the rare early single baffle globular muzzle brake that was also fitted to the Panzer IV F2.

Two American recovery lorries try to retrieve from the Normandy hedgerows the remains of an Ausf G bearing the unit number 201. The StuG has clearly thrown its tracks and the driving compartment armour has been penetrated.

This smouldering Ausf G belonged to the 17th SS-Panzergrenadier Division and was lost in the fighting in Normandy. The US 2nd Armored and 101st Airborne Divisions destroyed it during the German counter-attack on Carentan on 13 June 1944. The Germans got to within 500m of the town before they were repulsed.

Opposite above:
Men of the US 3rd Armored Division witness the fate of a hapless *Sturmartillerie* crewman who failed to escape his StuG Ausf G during the battle for Normandy.

Opposite below:
GIs pose at the roadside with the remains of another Ausf G. It has been completely wrecked.

The front of this StuG III gives a good indication of the texturing created by the anti-magnetic Zimmerit coating, as well as showing the additional bolt-on armour around the driver's vision port. The Zimmerit coating – a light grey plaster – was applied in the factory to the vertical surfaces of the hulls and turrets of most panzers and assault guns from early 1943. A tool was used to rake the paste, creating various ridged, stippled and criss-cross patterns before painting.

An abandoned StuG III somewhere in Normandy. It seems to have become stranded in a bomb crater.

This well-known shot shows a devastated Ausf G caught by Allied fighter-bombers while trying to escape the Falaise pocket in August 1944. It was attacked on the back roads near Nécy and its superstructure torn open by the blast.

This pristine Ausf F/8 is preserved at the Belgrade Military Museum in Serbia.

Chapter Three

Sturmgeschütz III Ausf G

The Ausf G was the last production Sturmgeschütz based on the Panzer III and proved to be by far the most numerous and therefore the most common. It is certainly the most photographed StuG variant. In total, 7,720 were built from December 1942 to March 1945, and in addition 173 were converted from Panzer III gun tanks in 1944. This large production run was due to the StuG III absorbing the Panzer III manufacturing facilities once the latter was completely phased out. Although the Ausf G went into production in 1942 and remained so until early 1945, by the end of the war there had been no major visual design changes except for the gun mantlet.

By the time the Ausf G began to roll off the assembly lines it had been decided to phase out the Panzer III altogether and replace it with the Panzer V Panther. This naturally caused complications with existing plans and was not a straightforward process. It was not simply a case of shutting down production and switching over immediately to a new vehicle. As a result the order for 1,000 Panzer Mk III Ausf M was reduced to 250. In addition, the Ausf N, armed with a short 75mm gun, had superseded the Ausf M. Therefore 165 Ausf M chassis were used for StuG Ausf G production from February to November 1943. The following year 173 Panzer IIIs were returned from the front line to Alkett for conversion to Ausf G.

The hull of the StuG Ausf G was the same as that used on the F/8. The main changes concerned differences in the superstructure. The sides were slanted and slanted plates were included to protect the front of both side panniers. A simple commander's cupola with periscopes was installed, as well as a much-needed shield for the machine gun in front of the gunner's hatch.

Photographic evidence shows that there were at least two types of cupola, one with vertical sides and another with a cast sloping front rising up from the superstructure roof. The latter was undoubtedly an improvement to counter the cupola front being a potential shot trap. Likewise, photographic evidence of StuGs in Italy and Normandy shows that not all Ausf G were fitted with the cupola, instead retaining the same hatch arrangement as the earlier Ausf F.

The fabricated box-like mantlet used on the Ausf F and initial Ausf G was supplemented in 1943 by an improved single-piece cast type known as the Topfblende (pot mantlet) or Saukopfblende (sow or pig's head mantlet). This was a smooth conical casting that had much better shot deflection qualities. The previous one tended to trap enemy rounds under the barrel, while the top of the mantlet could flick rounds onto the barrel or nose plates. Photographic evidence shows that the front of the box was vulnerable and could come off when struck with sufficient force to shear the retaining bolts.

Also in 1943 a coat of textured anti-magnetic paste was added to the hull and superstructure. Similarly, in an act of desperation or simply wartime expediency, some vehicles had their front armour strengthened by a layer of concrete up to 15cm deep on the armoured roof of the driver's compartment. The close-in defence of the Ausf G was enhanced with the installation of a coaxial machine gun, a remote control machine gun on the superstructure roof and the Nähverteidigungswaffe (close-in defence weapon). Those vehicles used to equip the remote-control companies were fitted with an additional radio aerial on the left front of the fighting compartment.

At the start of Hitler's ill-fated Kursk offensive against the Red Army on the Eastern Front in the summer of 1943 there were twenty-eight independent Sturmgeschütz detachments, four divisional StuG detachments, two remote control companies and twelve StuG platoons with the weak Luftwaffe field divisions.

General Heinz Guderian was far from a fan of the StuG Ausf G or the howitzer-armed StuH42. At the end of 1942 he observed, 'The construction of the Panzer III was now entirely discontinued, the industrial capacity thus freed being given over to the building of assault guns. The production figure for assault guns was to reach 220 per month by June 1943, of which twenty-four were to be armed with light field howitzers. This gun, with its low muzzle velocity and its very high trajectory, was undoubtedly well suited to the requirements of the infantry, but its production resulted in a fresh weakening of our defensive power against hostile tanks.'

By 1944–45 the StuG III Ausf G crews found themselves acting and looking increasingly like panzertruppen. The reality is that by this point in the war the distinction between the role of the Sturmgeschütz, Panzerjäger, Jagdpanzer and other self-propelled guns had become largely blurred. Increasingly they were called upon to fulfil the role traditionally carried out by the panzers, with many so-called panzer battalions being equipped with assault guns.

As explained in the Introduction, the assault gun crews were a breed apart and belonged to the artillery and not the Panzerwaffe. To emphasise this fact the assault gun brigades were renamed assault artillery brigades. This meant they were not permitted to wear the black panzertruppen uniform (although in practice this did not stop them).

The artillery vehicle crews wore a field-grey version; the collar patches were the same shape as those of the panzer crews, but were field grey piped with artillery red Waffenfarbe with metal skulls. They also initially wore a field-grey version of the Schutzmütze padded black panzer beret, but this was later replaced by a field-grey Feldmütze (side cap) or Einheitsfeldmütze (field cap).

The Panzerjäger units also initially wore the field-grey uniform, but from 1944 those serving with panzer and panzergrenadier divisions were instructed to wear black. Those serving with infantry and mountain divisions remained grey. A third style of uniform was introduced in mid-1942 with the reed-green panzer denim suit issued to Army armoured formations as working attire. This was worn over the panzertruppen black uniform or as a uniform in its own right.

As the Wehrmacht was driven back, the crews could only wear what was available from the quartermasters and they often did not have a choice in the matter. Toward the end of the war Sturmartillerie crews were known to wear the black panzer uniform or a combination of black and grey. It is quite possible that they also ended up with the panzer denims as well.

This Ausf G captured by the Americans in France in 1944 is from the production run that retained the distinctive Ausf F bolted box gun mantlet. Key features on the G model were the inclusion of a commander's cupola with periscopes and slanted sides on the superstructure. This particular vehicle, numbered 232, is coated in anti-magnetic Zimmerit paste, as is the one next to it, which has been finished in a criss-cross pattern.

Interestingly, the crew of this captured Ausf G attempted to up-armour the hull by attaching spare track links between the return rollers and the wheels. Spare road wheels are stored on the rear of the engine deck. This side profile shot gives a clear view of the new commander's cupola. The Ausf G was built by Alkett and MIAG from December 1942 until the end of the war.

Two Ausf G on patrol on the Eastern Front. The lead vehicle has been fitted with armoured side skirts (Schürzen). These plates consisted of mild steel boiler plating fitted to rails with the intention of protecting the vehicle's armour against hollow charge projectiles. The first StuG has either a two- or three-tone camouflage scheme applied to the Schürzen and the glacis plate.

Sturmartillerie crews take a break by a column of StuG III Ausf G. This vehicle has been camouflaged with the application of foliage and a disruptive pattern on its *Schürzen*.

An Ausf G and panzergrenadiers rounding up dejected Soviet prisoners on the Eastern Front.

Transporting armoured fighting vehicles by train could be hazardous in the face of air attack. The explosion that wrecked this train was such that it blew the Ausf G from its flatcar. This vehicle is fitted with the external remote machine gun mounting on the roof, although the machine gun is not installed. The cupola also appears to feature a deflection slope at the front.

The roof of the superstructure on this Ausf G has been torn off. Any crew inside would have been killed instantly, but the glacis hatches are open suggesting that the vehicle had already been abandoned. Such destruction was often caused by the ammunition 'cooking off', rather than by a direct hit. The Zimmerit has been finished in a crisscross pattern.

British troops give captured enemy equipment in Italy the once-over. In the foreground are two StuG III Ausf G, then two Marder III self-propelled anti-tank guns and two Italian Semovente assault guns. The vehicle nearest the camera had the Saukopfblende one-piece cast gun mantlet which was introduced in late 1943. Both StuGs have up-armoured superstructure thanks to the installation of spare wheel racks.

This and the next two photographs show different views of a column of six abandoned Ausf G on the Eastern Front. The lead vehicle has been rear-ended by the one behind it. Both StuGs are coated in stippled Zimmerit and the superstructure has been up-armoured with steel plating (possibly discarded Schürzen) and the application of spare track links and road wheels.

Above and opposite:
Some of the StuGs, including the lead vehicle, have the newer Saukopf mantlet, while others have the Ausf F variant. The front vehicle has the sloping front cupola. These assault guns may have been caught by Red Air Force Shturmovik ground-attack aircraft and abandoned at the roadside.

Factory-fresh Ausf F, painted in dunkel gelb (sand-yellow), heading for the front.

Ausf G photographed in Italy. The middle vehicle is clearly coated in Zimmerit and has Schürzen fitted on its left-hand side (the right-hand side equivalent has probably been accidentally torn off or battle-damaged). The central Sturmartillerie crewman is wearing the Feldmütze (side cap), while the man on the right is wearing the Einheitsmütze (field cap).

American troops from the US 28th Infantry Division clamber over a wrecked Ausf G. It has lost its tracks and two road wheels; the idler and muzzle brake also appear damaged.

Czech civilians at Gävle Brod rummage through the debris surrounding an abandoned up-armoured Ausf G.

1SS Pz Div

This drowned Ausf G belonging to the 1st SS Panzer Division ended up in the Orne river at Putanges (south of Falaise) during the German retreat in Normandy in August 1944. The divisional symbol is just visible on the right-hand track guard. It was serving with SS-Sturmgeschütz Abteilung 1. A towline is attached, suggesting that it may have been under tow, but it is not clear if it was pushed or accidentally fell into the water.

This German vehicle dump was in the American sector near Isigny-sur-Mer in Normandy. Just behind the Sd Kfz 251 half-track bearing an Allied star is a StuG III Ausf G with Saukopfblende.

Somewhere in Germany was the final resting-place for this hull-down Ausf G. Note the shot trap eliminator, just in front of the cupola, that slopes up from the roof to just beneath the periscopes mounting. The V-shaped object on the roof to the left is the remote-controlled machine gun station.

These two photographs show an armoured vehicle dump in Germany containing at least five battle-damaged Ausf G. They all have the Saukopf mantlet, but lack Zimmerit as this practice ceased from mid-1944. None of them is equipped with Schürzen.

Chapter Four

Sturmhaubitze 42

The Sturmhaubitze 42 was a heavy assault StuG variant armed with a 105mm howitzer. This armoured fighting vehicle was developed because the StuG units realised they needed heavier fire support when fighting alongside infantry. Despite a shaky start, over 1,200 of these were built from October 1942 to February 1945.

As early as 1941 there had been moves to produce a heavy fire support assault gun. Initial attempts involved marrying the 150mm Stu I G L/11 gun (or SiG33) to the Panzer III chassis. The resulting Sturminfanteriegeschütz 33B (assault infantry gun, StuIG33B or SiG33B for short) was the third installation of the SiG33 on a panzer chassis. However, those fitted to the Panzer I and II chassis had open fighting compartments and, like the SiG33B, were only ever built in very small numbers.

Alkett was instructed in July 1941 to provide twelve Panzer III chassis to take the 150mm gun, which were to be completed by mid-September. While the SiG33B utilised the StuG Ausf E and F/8 hull, the superstructure had to be completely redesigned to create a very boxy looking fully enclosed fighting compartment for the much larger gun. The main armament was mounted in a sliding gun mantlet offset to the right. Secondary armament was supplied by an MG34 mounted in the right-hand side of the superstructure's front.

Delays resulted in the initial version being finished in late 1941 and early 1942. Then on 20 September 1942 another order was placed for twelve assault vehicles, capable of smashing houses, to be completed in two weeks. The original batch of SiG33B were rebuilt and twelve new ones were constructed in October 1942, bringing the total number built to just twenty-four.

In November 1942 a heavy StuG company was deployed to Stalingrad to add punch to the panzer and panzergrenadier divisions. A second company was formed as part of the 201st Panzer Regiment serving with the 23rd Panzer Division. This formation was sent to try to break the Red Army's stranglehold on the German 6th Army trapped at Stalingrad in the winter of 1942/3.

Another attempt to design a heavily armed assault gun involved mounting the leFH18 105mm light field howitzer in a trial series of twelve StuGs to run from January to March 1942. This gun was the German Army's standard towed divisional field piece, but it was rather heavy and not as mobile as the gunners would have liked. Due to a number of setbacks just a single prototype was completed in March 1942, with five Sturmhaubitze (StuH) built on StuG Ausf F and another four on StuG F/8 chassis finished in October 1942.

Delivery of the first production series of the StuH42 did not commence until March 1943, with the highest monthly output attained in September 1944 with 199 vehicles. These were armed with the StuH42 L/28 105mm gun fitted with a muzzle brake, similar to the leFH18(M), to allow it to fire more powerful ammunition, thus giving it greater range.

The Ausf F, F/8 and G were used to produce the StuH42, so the hull and superstructure were the same. The only real difference was the altered gun mount to take the bigger weapon; similarly the internal storage had to be changed to take the larger rounds. Like the Ausf G, late production models of the StuH42 also included a coaxial mount for a machine gun. Some late production StuH42 lacked a muzzle brake and were fitted with a remote control machine gun. Those based on the StuG Ausf G had the Saukopf gun mantlet.

When the battle of Kursk started, the German Army Groups Centre and South had sixty-eight StuH42. From 1943 the StuH were issued to the StuG detachments that became full brigades. Each unit was supplied with nine StuH42 to support the Ausf F and G by providing heavier firepower and supplementing close range anti-tank defence.

A final armed support variant in the assault gun family was the Sturmgeschütz (Fl) flame-thrower. These were extremely limited in number, with just ten converted in May and June 1943. The ending of Panzer III production resulted in just a hundred tanks being available for the Flammpanzer (flame-throwing tank) programme. To compensate for this it was proposed that ten of the 220 StuGs due for delivery in June 1943 would be armed with the 14mm Flammenwerfer, which was also installed in the Panzer III (Fl). Photographic evidence shows that the Ausf F/8 was used as the base vehicle. The Flammenwerfer replaced the 75mm Sturmkanone and flame fuel tanks were installed, otherwise the appearance was that of a standard StuG. The range of the flame-thrower was 55–60m.

Two views of the StuH42 based on the StuG III Ausf G. The Ausf F was also armed with the StuH42 105mm light field howitzer. The only real difference between the assault howitzer and the assault gun variants was the length and diameter of the barrel. The short stubby 105mm gun did not extend very far beyond the glacis plate. The second shot shows additional armour bolted to the nose plates and the front vertical plate.

This StuG appears to be a badly damaged late model StuH42 Ausf F without the double baffle muzzle brake. During the battle of Kursk in 1943 the Germans deployed sixty-eight of these vehicles to help deal with Soviet defences.

Another late model StuH42 Ausf F abandoned in the snow. The barrel length suggests it may possibly be a regular Ausf F missing its muzzle brake. The first 119 StuG Ausf F fitted with the StuK40 L/43 were produced without muzzle brakes.

A late model StuH42 Ausf F destroyed in the fighting in northwest Europe in 1944–45.

The gun on this StuG III Ausf G is so badly damaged that it is difficult to tell whether it was armed with a 75mm or 105mm gun.

The driver's hatch on the glacis plate was very small, and just sufficient for him to poke his head out when driving. In combat the driver would rely on the vision port.

A StuG III Ausf G and a Panther tank near Nettuno, Italy, March 1944.

Sturmartillerie crew and panzertruppen pose with a StuG III near Monte Cassino, during the Italian campaign in the spring of 1944.

Opposite:
Two shots of a well concealed StuG III supporting German paratroops at Monte Cassino, Italy, in 1944.

61

61

An American jeep makes its way between a burning M4 Sherman and a knocked-out StuG III during the fighting in Normandy in 1944.

This StuG III Ausf G with *Schürzen* was photographed somewhere on the Eastern Front.

StuG III with additional 30mm frontal armour bolted to the nose plate.

Chapter Five

Sturmgeschütz IV and Jagdpanzer IV

In light of the slow rate of production for the Tiger heavy tank and the unwelcome teething problems experienced with the Panther medium tank, Guderian, as Inspector General of Armoured Troops, appreciated that the Panzerwaffe remained very reliant on the Panzer IV. During the summer of 1943, following a visit to the Eastern Front, Guderian became ill with dysentery. He recalled, 'Meanwhile during my absence an attempt had been made to stop producing Panzer IVs and to build assault guns in their place. The Todt Organisation, which was building the Atlantic Wall and other fortifications, proposed that tank turrets be built into pillboxes; in view of our limited production this would undoubtedly be a serious blow to our mobile tank forces and showed a complete lack of comprehension of the real situation.'

Hitler's armoured vehicle designers were looking at ways to improve, and ultimately replace, the tried and tested StuG III. Events soon forced their hand. Fortunately for Hitler, but much to Guderian's displeasure, trials had already been conducted into the feasibility of marrying the StuG III superstructure to the Panzer IV chassis. Guderian was of the view that the StuG III was more than adequate and did not need replacing. He could understand the utility of employing the Panzer III factories to build StuGs, though he would have preferred them to be converted to Panzer IV production.

Guderian was understandably annoyed because in April 1943 he had gained agreement that Panzer IV production would continue and be expanded during 1943–44 until mass production of the Panther could be assured. He was therefore far from happy about the development of the forthcoming StuG IV and Jagdpanzer IV as he saw them as an unwanted distraction. He recorded,

In October [1943] tank production suffered further in favour of the production of assault guns: Panzer IVs were diverted to carrying the 75mm

L/70 cannon and Panthers [Jagdpanthers] the long 88mm L/71. . . . the actual result was simply a decrease in the production of the only useful combat tank available to us at the time, the Panzer IV; and furthermore it was only in this month that the production figures for that tank reached the really very modest total of 100.

Allied bombers played a part in Hitler's decision to press ahead with the StuG IV. The Alkett factory building the StuG III was bombed in late November 1943, severely disrupting output. Hitler wanted the shortfall remedied as quickly as possible, which meant that part of the Krupp works at Magdeburg was instructed to manufacture the StuG IV. Hitler was shown a StuG IV on 16 December 1943 and he insisted it go into production immediately. Hitler and his staff were in part swayed by combat reports showing that the Panzer IV was struggling to hold its own. In addition, it was imperative that losses suffered at Kursk be made good, and as assault guns were easier to build, it seemed a preferable and swifter solution.

The vital Krupp tank plant halted Panzer IV production in early December 1943 and in the New Year went over completely to manufacturing the StuG IV. The first thirty were produced from chassis supplied by the Nibelungenwerke from its regular tank production line.

Utilising the battle-proven Panzer Mk IV chassis, the StuG IV assault gun was armed with the 75mm StuK40 L/48 gun and the Jagdpanzer IV tank destroyer with the 75mm Pak39 L/48. The 75mm L/70 gun noted by Guderian was actually fitted to the Panzer IV/70 designed as the Jagdpanzer IV's eventual replacement. Almost 1,140 StuG IVs were built between December 1943 and March 1945, and 769 Jagdpanzer IVs from January to November 1944. The latter first went into action in Italy with the Hermann Göring Division.

The Panzer IV-based assault guns and tank destroyers were easily recognisable as they had eight road wheels and four return rollers, whereas the Panzer III had six and three respectively. On the StuG IV the driver's position was relocated to an armoured cab equipped with two periscopes but no vision port, and with an access hatch in the roof rather than in the glacis. It was up-armoured from its predecessor by the application of 15cm-thick concrete slabs fitted to the front of the superstructure and the driver's cab, hence the loss of the vision port.

In early 1944 the cast Saukopfblende was introduced and in the summer the external machine gun shield, used by the loader, was upgraded to a remote controlled machine gun mount and a Nähverteidigungswaffe close-defence weapon was installed on the roof. The StuG IV was issued to the artillery's StuG brigades, plus the Panzerjäger detachments of the panzer and infantry divisions.

Built by Vomag, the Jagdpanzer IV first appeared in early 1944. It had been developed as a specific replacement for the StuG III. Hitler had been shown a soft steel model in October 1943 and a final prototype at the end of the year. Initially (until May 1944) Vomag produced the Jagdpanzer IV and the Panzer IV side-by-side until the factory went completely over to Jagdpanzer IV production.

While the Jagdpanzer had the same basic chassis, suspension and drive train as the gun tank from which it was derived, the hull front was redesigned. Two plates forming a sharp nose replaced the vertical front plate and the superstructure had sloping sides. The upper hull and superstructure front armour was increased to 80mm and the sides to 40mm in May 1944. The main armament was flanked by two machine gun ports.

From March 1944 the Jagdpanzer IV was issued to the Panzerjäger units of the panzer divisions. They first saw combat in Italy and then with the 4th and 5th Panzer Divisions on the Eastern Front and with Panzer Lehr, 9th Panzer and the 12th SS in Normandy. Despite Guderian's concerns over the German Army's dwindling tank fleet, Panzer IV production was also given over to the Panzer IV/70 tank destroyer in the summer of 1944. This was at the very point that Army Group Centre was collapsing on the Eastern Front and Army Group B was being defeated in France.

A GI takes a closer look at a StuG IV destroyed near Périers on 24 July 1944 by the US Army. It has the standard Zimmerit coating applied to both the hull and the superstructure. This vehicle probably served with the 2nd SS Panzer Division or the 17th SS Panzergrenadier Division. This type of StuG was rare in Normandy, with most tank destroyer battalions and some SS-Panzer companies equipped mainly with the StuG III Ausf G.

A StuG IV belonging to the 1st SS Panzer Division being inspected by men of the US 1st Infantry Division on 29 July 1944 near Marigny, 5 miles southeast of Périers. The vehicle has shed its left track.

A StuG IV bearing the unit ID number '115'. This vehicle appears undamaged and seems to have been abandoned at the roadside. The lack of Zimmerit indicates that it is a late production model. Like the StuG III, the StuG IV was employed both as an assault gun supporting the infantry and as a dedicated tank destroyer.

This preserved StuG IV (at the Armoured Warfare Museum in Poznan, Poland) highlights the key differences from the StuG III; most notably the Panzer IV running gear is longer, with two additional road wheels and an extra return roller. In addition, the up-armoured superstructure lacks a driver's vision port, leaving the driver reliant on two periscopes.

Another StuG IV abandoned at the roadside in France. Note the rubber wheel rim propped against the drive sprocket.

The final resting place for this StuG IV belonging to the 17th SS Panzergrenadier Division was a ditch in France in 1944. It may have parked here in an ambush position or been knocked out and then unceremoniously shunted off the road. The Zimmerit has been chipped off the side of the superstructure, possibly indicating impact marks.

StuG IVs also saw combat in Italy, where there was always a shortage of panzers. The destruction of this vehicle was so violent that the blast lifted the StuK40 75mm gun and *Saukopf* mantlet clear of the superstructure.

Left, opposite above and below:
This series of photos shows Sturmartillerietruppen posing with a StuG IV at Mielau in Poland. The vehicle is fitted with Schürzen but the left-hand front plate is missing. The men are wearing field-grey Einheitsfeldmütze but much darker denim overalls.

Belonging to Sturmartillerie Brigade 277, this StuG IV was destroyed by the Red Army in East Prussia in February 1945. This unit started life in February 1944 as Sturmgeschütz Brigade 277 and was redesignated 'Sturmartillerie' in December 1944. It fought with both the 3rd and 4th Panzer Armies.

American troops cautiously check the battered remains of a StuG V, as there was always the risk of booby-traps left to catch the unwary. The second and sixth wheels are missing, as are the tracks. The raised flap at the back is the engine compartment cover.

This pre-production Jagdpanzer IV is preserved at the Panzermuseum, Munster, Germany. Hitler was presented with a soft steel model in October 1943 and a final prototype in December 1943. The Jagdpanzer IV was intended to replace the StuG III but ended up being produced alongside the latter and the Panzer IV/40 tank destroyer.

The Panzermuseum also has a production Jagdpanzer IV fitted with Schürzen and coated in Zimmerit.

Chapter Six

Panzer IV/70 (V) and 70 (A)

The Panzer IV/70(V) tank destroyer went into production in August 1944, in parallel with the StuG IV and Jagdpanzer IV, and ran until the end of the war, by which time 930 had been produced. Its key combat role was supporting Hitler's Ardennes Offensive in December 1944. Some 278 Panzer IV/70(A) models were also built during the same period and fought on the Eastern Front. While similar in appearance to the StuG IV and especially the Jagdpanzer IV, the Panzer IV/70 variants lacked a muzzle brake on their main gun.

The Panzer IV/70(V) was Vomag's improved version of its Jagdpanzer IV, with the PaK42 L/70 75mm gun replacing the Pak39 L/48 of its predecessor. It went into production in the summer of 1944 alongside the Vomag Jagdpanzer, until the latter was completely replaced in December 1944. The Panzer IV/70(V)'s longer gun and 80mm frontal armour made it quite nose-heavy, which meant that the rubber-tyred road wheels suffered excessive wear. To remedy this problem, on later production models the first two wheel stations were fitted with all steel-rimmed wheels. Also the later models had only three return rollers, in keeping with the savings made on the Panzer IV Ausf J – the final production model of the Panzer IV.

The Panzer IV/70(V) was issued to the 105th and 106th Independent Panzer Brigades in the summer of 1944. Other tank brigades, along with independent Panzerjäger units and those assigned to the panzer divisions, were likewise equipped with this new tank destroyer. In the winter of 1944/5 a total of 137 Panzer IV/70(V) were available for Hitler's surprise Ardennes Offensive against the American Army.

Alkett, while pressing on with StuG III and StuH42 production, also became involved in Guderian's unwanted distraction from tank building. The Panzer IV/70(A) was the Alkett variant of the Panzer IV tank destroyer and was produced at the Nibelungenwerke alongside the Panzer IV Ausf J. Like the Vomag version, it was armed with the 75mm PaK42 gun and both variants were built simultaneously until the end of the war.

The Panzer IV/70(A) utilised the Panzer IV chassis and was very similar in appearance to the Panzer IV/70(V), with both using the same type of gun mount and mantlet. However, the superstructure was stepped where it was fitted to the hull, with vertical edges to the lower front and sides. As a result, while the Panzer IV/70(V) was the same height as the Jagdpanzer IV at 1.85m, the Alkett version was considerably higher at 2.35m. This made the Panzer IV(A) taller than the StuG III and StuG IV.

Alkett's tank destroyer also suffered with nose-weight problems, which again necessitated using steel-rimmed road wheels at the front. Most of the Panzer IV/70(A) were deployed to the Eastern Front; a few, though, were encountered by the Western Allies, with the French Army capturing at least one example. Tellingly, its frontal armour had been penetrated in the upper part of the raised superstructure.

In late 1944 the Panzer IV/70 was used to equip the tank destroyer unit of each panzer division; this normally comprised twenty-one vehicles. On the eve of the Ardennes Offensive the 1st SS Panzer Division's SS-Panzerjäger Abteilung I had only half its complement. These supported Kampfgruppe Hansen in the fighting at Poteau and then moved to assist Kampfgruppe Peiper.

At Petit-Spai some of the 1st SS's Panzer IV/70 reached the southern bank of the Amblève river, but the bridge there was not capable of taking the vehicle's 25 tons. Despite SS-Hauptsturmführer Otto Holt's objections, his Panzer IV/70 company was ordered to cross. As a result, his lead vehicle crashed through the bridge and into the river. The end of the shattered bridge created a vertical barrier in front of Holt. His Panzer IV/70 flooded and remained trapped in the water until captured by the Americans.

Clearly Guderian was not a fan of the StuG IV, the Jagdpanzer IV or the Panzer IV/70. In his view vital tank output diverted to numerous types of assault gun and tank destroyer production wasted over 3,100 Panzer IVs that would have been better employed issued to the panzer divisions.

Built by Vomag, the Panzer IV(V) was based on the Panzer IV. This is a late production model using the Ausf J chassis with the three return rollers. It was photographed in December 1944 and has the ambush pattern camouflage scheme, consisting of olivgrun (olive green) over the factory finish dunkel gelb (deep sand yellow) with spots of dunkel gelb over the olivgrun. The scheme may in fact be three-tone and may include patches of rotbraun (reddish brown).

Hitler massed 137 Panzer IV/70 for his 1944/5 winter offensive on the Western Front. This one has had its superstructure completely shattered. The chassis is that of the Ausf J. The first two wheels have thin steel rims; these were fitted because the vehicle was nose-heavy and wore out rubber-tyred wheels very quickly.

Two Panzer IV/70(V), destroyed in the fighting on the Western Front, being examined by curious GIs.

These Panzer IV/70(V) Ausf J, abandoned outside Oberpleis in Germany and photographed in March 1945, have neither Zimmerit nor *Schürzen*. Both are sporting an indistinct two-tone camouflage scheme and a faint tactical number is just visible on the superstructure of the nearest vehicle.

These two Panzer IV/70(V) were involved in the fighting in Hungary in 1945 when Hitler launched a massive counter-offensive.

A Panzer IV/70(V) and a StuG III on the streets of Berlin.

A Panzer IV/70(V) knocked out on the Eastern Front.

Hungarian PoWs file past a Panzer IV/70(V) lost during the fighting for Budapest.

Alkett's version of the Panzer IV/70 was distinguishable by the stepped front and sides on the superstructure, which was almost half a metre higher than its Vomag counterpart. Fewer than 300 Panzer IV/70(A) were built.

Above, opposite above and below:
This Panzer IV/70(A) belonging to Panzer Regiment 2 was captured by the French Army near Rudlin, France, in 1944, and ended up in the Saumur Tank Museum. Its armour has been penetrated on the front of the superstructure.

A StuG III Ausf F somewhere on the Eastern Front. It lacks both Zimmerit and *Schürzen*.

A StuG III Ausf G on manoeuvres. The muzzle brake cover indicates that the crew are not expecting trouble. The vehicle is painted in dunkel gelb (deep sand yellow) with olivgrun (olive green) or rotbraun (reddish brown) camouflage.

Chapter Seven

Panzerjäger Marder I, II and III

hree types of Marder self-propelled anti-tank gun were created, employing French, German and Czech tracked chassis, as a stopgap measure for the infantry. The latter type, dubbed Marder III, also resulted in three different variants, the last of which was quite successful. The name Marder is German for the marten, a member of the weasel family, and may in part have been chosen to reflect how small the vehicle was and yet how deadly.

The early Marder I was constructed by mounting a 75mm PaK40/1 gun in an open fighting compartment on the rear of a captured French Lorraine Schlepper (f) or Tracteur Blindé tracked carrier. In total, 170 were converted by Major Alfred Becker in Paris to the Panzerjäger role and a number were also converted to self-propelled artillery using 105mm and 150mm guns. A number of the latter ended up in North Africa with Rommel's troops. Thanks to Becker's engineering expertise, the Geschützwagen (gun motor carriage) Lorraine Schlepper (f) (Sd Kfz 135) was created in the summer of 1942 and most were issued to units in France. About 130 Marder I saw combat during the battle for Normandy.

The Marder I was woefully slow and under-armoured. It could barely manage 30km/hr and had just 10mm of armour on the front and sides. This was worse than the Panzerjäger I. The fighting compartment on the Marder I was also very cramped. By contrast, the Marder II was capable of 40km/hr and had 30mm of frontal armour and 15mm on the sides. The subsequent first two versions of the Marder III had a similar speed, but had 50mm of armour on the front and 15mm on the sides. However, the angle of deflection on these vehicles was poorer. The final version of the Marder III again suffered from thin armour but had better deflection angles.

The Germans also converted a very limited number of captured French Hotchkiss H-39 and FCM36 light tanks into self-propelled anti-tank guns armed with the ubiquitous PaK40. Just twenty-four 75mm PaK40(Sf) auf Geschützwagen 39H(f) and ten 75mm PaK40(Sf) auf Geschützwagen FCM(f) were converted in 1942 and

1943 respectively. These also saw action in France in 1944. A number of both chassis were additionally converted to carry the 105mm howitzer.

An earlier conversion, employing the captured Renault R-35 light tank and captured Czech 47mm anti-tank gun, was largely restricted to security duties in France. It was similar to the Panzerjäger I, which appeared in 1940 and utilised the same gun as mounted on converted Panzer I Ausf B. This self-propelled anti-tank gun was phased out in late 1943.

In Normandy the 21st Panzer Division's organisation was almost unique; unlike the other panzer divisions (with the exception of the 10th SS), it had no Panther tank battalion, just Panzer IVs. Instead, it had an assault gun battalion and an anti-tank battalion with towed guns. The 2nd Battalion of Panzer Regiment 22 was equipped with a variety of captured French tanks, while Panzer Artillery Regiment 155 and Sturmgeschütz Battalion 200 were armed with self-propelled guns converted from French tanks. The latter, under Major Becker, were not in reality Sturmgeschütz as they had open fighting compartments and could not really function as assault guns. Moreover, the additional armour meant these vehicles were perilously overloaded and were unable to engage Allied tanks on anything like equal terms.

In the face of Operation Goodwood, launched on 18 July 1944, Major Becker's five batteries from Sturmgeschütz Battalion 200 were deployed at Démouville, Giberville, Grentheville and the farms of le Mensil-Frémentel and le Prieuré, supported by Colonel Hans von Luck's Panzergrenadiers. On the eastern half of the battlefield they represented the Germans' only mobile tactical reserve. These forces attempted to hold up the British tanks, but those guns at Démouville were lost in the opening British bombardment.

Becker's battery at Giberville withdrew to the northwest of Bras, and along with the guns at Grentheville shelled British tanks to the east and west. The two batteries at the farms, lacking infantry protection, were also soon forced back by the relentless tide of Allied tanks. The remains of Becker's assault gun battalion engaged the British 29th Brigade's lead regiment, the Fife & Forfar Yeomanry, destroying more than twenty Shermans before conducting a fighting withdrawal towards the 1st SS Panzer Division's 'stop line' on the strategically vital Bourguébus ridge. By the end of the day most of Becker's so-called assault guns were burning wrecks.

The initial model Marder II, designated the Sd Kfz 132, which looked very similar to the first version of the Marder III, was produced as a stopgap measure using the Panzer II Ausf D and E chassis built by MAN. The latter differed from the FAMO Panzer II Ausf A, B, C and F chassis in that they had only four double road wheels instead of the five singles, and lacked the four return rollers. This Marder II was armed with a captured Russian 76.2mm gun. During Operation Barbarossa the

German Army had captured thousands of Russian FK296, which was designated the PaK36(r) and rechambered to take the PaK40 anti-tank round. Alkett and Wegmann converted 201 of these vehicles from April 1942 to June 1943. The type was mainly deployed on the Eastern Front and was phased out of front-line service in early 1944 once adequate numbers of Marder III had been produced.

A second and more numerous variant of the Marder II (Sd Kfz 131) consisted of a German 75mm PaK40/2 gun installed in an open-top fighting compartment in the middle of a Panzer II Ausf F chassis. From June 1942 to June 1943 the manufacturers FAMO, MAN and Daimler-Benz built a total of 576 Marder II. Production was stopped in favour of the Wespe self-propelled light field howitzer armed with the 105mm leFH18(M) gun. Another seventy-five were converted from existing Panzer II from July 1943 to March 1944. Marder II were issued to the Panzerjäger detachments from July 1942 and saw action in all the major theatres of operation.

It is said that 'necessity is the mother of all invention' and this was certainly the case with Rommel's anti-tank requirements in North Africa and those of the Wehrmacht on the Eastern Front. What was essentially a quick fix utilising a Russian gun and a Czech tank chassis resulted in the highly successful Marder III series of self-propelled tank hunters. Once it was clear that the captured Czech PzKpfw 38(t) light tank was obsolete as a battle tank and too slow for a reconnaissance role, it was decided to utilise the robust and highly reliable chassis as a gun carriage. A number of these tanks had their turrets removed and a Russian 7.62mm gun installed into an open fighting compartment.

After a prototype Marder III had been produced in late December 1941, it was decreed that from the end of March 1942 some seventeen Panzerjäger 38(t) (Sd Kfz 139) were to be built, rising to thirty a month by mid-year. Between April and October 1942 some 344 of these Panzerjäger self-propelled guns were built, with another nineteen converted from existing Panzer 38(t) in 1943 by Böhmisch-Mährische Maschinenfabrik (BMM), the Czech armoured fighting vehicle manufacturer in Prague (formerly Ceskomoravska Kolben Danel – CKD or Praga). The bulk of them were issued to units on the Eastern Front. Rommel also received sixty-six in North Africa that were issued to two Panzerjäger battalions.

While this Panzerjäger provided a very welcome stopgap, it was far from perfect. The gun was placed on top of the hull superstructure and forward of the rear-mounted engine, which gave the vehicle a very high profile. In fact, at 2.5m it was fractionally higher than the original tank, which left the gunners very exposed.

In June 1942 another prototype Marder III was produced. Armed with the German 75mm PaK40/3 anti-tank gun, it included an improved superstructure for the fighting compartment, which was larger, squatter, lighter and gave the crew better protection. The height, however, was the same at 2.5m. Essentially the 7.5cm

PaK40/3 auf Panzerkampfwagen 38(t) Ausf H (Sd Kfz 138) looked the same as its predecessor but the side armour of the superstructure sloped back towards the engine. It went into production in November 1942 and by April 1943 BMM had built 242, while a further 175 were converted from existing Panzer 38(t). This type of Panzerjäger was issued to Army, Waffen-SS and Luftwaffe ground units serving on the Eastern Front, in Tunisia and in Italy.

The initial model of the Marder, armed with the Russian gun, was built using the Ausf G Panzer 38(t) chassis. Subsequently it and the PaK40 variant were built using the Ausf H. There was also a third version using the Ausf M. It was recognised that the first two versions of the Marder III were not ideal and that a new design was needed. In July 1942 Hitler ordered that the Panzer 38(t) be switched over entirely to self-propelled gun production.

On the final version of the Panzerjäger 38(t) it was decided to place the engine in the middle of the hull, which allowed the fighting compartment and the gun to be located to the rear. Although less thickly armoured than its predecessors, the redesigned superstructure had much better deflection angles, greatly enhancing protection. The thinner armour also meant it was fractionally lighter than the two initial versions.

Whereas the first two variants retained the 38(t) light tank drive sprocket, idler, four wheels and two return rollers on either side, the Marder III Ausf M only had a single central return roller. A total of 975 Panzerjäger 38(t) with 7.5cm PaK40/3 Ausf M (Sd Kfz 138) were constructed by BMM between April 1943 and May 1944. Its manufacture then gave way to the Jagdpanzer 38(t) Hetzer (baiter).

The Marder III self-propelled anti-tank gun family, based on the 38(t) and Panzer II, saw extensive use with the Army and Waffen-SS. The Czech-built Marder IIIs equipping the tank hunter battalion of the 1st SS Panzer Division helped recapture Kharkov in March 1943 and subsequently paraded triumphantly through the streets in a show of strength. At the battle of Monte Cassino in Italy the 3rd Panzergrenadier Division deployed both the Czech Marder and Grille self-propelled guns against the Allies.

SS Kampfgruppen equipped with Marder IIIs also helped inflict a major setback on the British Army. When General Montgomery launched Operation Market Garden on 17 September 1944, it was intended to take the Allies over the Rhine and into the Ruhr – the Nazi industrial heartland. Although potentially a masterstroke, Market Garden was flawed, especially as the British airborne spearhead came up against recuperating elements of the 9th SS and 10th SS Panzer Divisions at Arnhem. The SS units were extremely under-strength but there could be only one outcome from pitting lightly armed paratroops against Marder, StuG III and Tiger tanks.

As well as providing welcome mobile anti-tank gun support to the Wehrmacht, the 38(t) chassis was also used for mobile artillery. Another self-propelled gun that was built in some numbers was the Grille or Bison, armed with a 150mm field gun. This was used to equip the panzergrenadier regiments within the panzer divisions and provided valuable support in Russia, Tunisia, Italy and Normandy. The self-propelled gun company of the 2nd SS Panzergrenadier Regiment, serving with Kampfgruppe Peiper during the 1944 Ardennes Offensive, included six Grille. They got as far as La Gleize, where their crews abandoned them.

The impact on the Wehrmacht of the little Skoda 38(t) and its subsequent German-designed variants was considerable, and the crews developed a healthy respect for its capabilities. In fact, Guderian became very concerned over Hitler's reliance on the Czech tanks. By 1942 the preoccupation had become the production of self-propelled guns rather than tanks, and to make matters worse the self-propelled guns were being armoured with unhardened steel.

Guderian recalled, 'the troops were already beginning to complain that a self-propelled gun on a Panzer II or Czech LT-38 chassis was not a sufficiently effective weapon'. But Hitler would not be swayed and the following year instructed that the production of the Czech tank and Panzer II be devoted solely to making chassis for self-propelled guns. General von Thoma, who was captured in North Africa, was also dismissive of the early hybrids. In criticising the Wehrmacht's conduct of the war on the Eastern Front, he noted, 'Another handicap was the defectiveness of our self-propelled artillery. This weapon is invaluable. But those we used were only makeshift, and the chassis was overloaded.'

French refugees hurry past a 75mm PaK40/1 auf Geschützwagen Lorraine Schlepper (f) or Marder I in Normandy in 1944. This consisted of a self-propelled anti-tank gun mounted on a captured French carrier chassis. This type of conversion was carried out in Paris and such vehicles were deployed with German units on garrison duty in France.

While the Marder I had a good anti-tank gun, it was woefully under-powered and under-armoured. These two shots show how crammed and exposed the five-man crew was.

Dubbed *Löwe* (lion) by its crew, this Marder I was photographed at a captured equipment dump south of Trevières in France in September 1944. It has been painted in all three colours of the German camouflage system, with the *dunkel gelb* main coat mostly over-painted in *olivgrun*. It also features a very prominent German cross.

Above, opposite above and below:
The Panzer Selbstfahrlatte I für 76.2mm PaK46(r) auf Fahrgestell Panzerkampfwagen II Ausf D and E (or LaS 762) – better known as the Marder II – went into production in April 1942 with the conversion of 200 Panzer II tanks into self-propelled anti-tank guns using captured Soviet weapons. The end result looked very much like the initial Marder III, based on the 38(t) light tank, which went into production at the same time. The Marder II provided a vital stopgap on the Eastern Front and was not phased out until early 1944.

The Marder II variant utilising the Panzer II A, B, C and F chassis and armed with a German PaK40 first appeared in June 1942, and 651 had been built by March 1944. The last batch was converted from existing tanks as Panzer II production went over to Wespe 105mm self-propelled gun production.

The first series Marder III, also known as the Panzerjäger 38(t) für 76.2mm PaK36(r) (Sd Kfz 139), utilised the Panzer 38(t) and a captured Soviet gun. It first went into production in Prague in April 1942. This one is in action on the Eastern Front and the crewman seems to be giving the gunner directions.

Rommel received sixty-six of the first series Marder III to support his operations in North Africa. Although it was well armed, its high profile and exposed fighting compartment proved far from ideal and left the crew vulnerable to direct and indirect fire.

Another first series Marder III captured in North Africa. They first arrived in May 1942 and served with Panzerjäger Battalion 33 supporting the 15th Panzer Division.

Above and opposite:
The second series Marder III was designated the 75mm PaK40/3 auf Panzerkampfwagen 38(t) Ausf H (Sd Kfz 138). It saw action with the 1st SS Panzer Division from December 1942. The first shot shows one captured by the Red Army. The Marder III Ausf H featured a redesigned superstructure.

A Marder III Ausf H destroyed in Italy. As in the previous model the fighting compartment was set forward of the engine, making it nose-heavy.

The third series Marder III, designated the Panzerjäger 38(t) mit 75mm PaK40/3 Ausf M (Sd Kfz 138) went into production in April 1943. These are late production vehicles, identifiable by the cast towing lugs at the front, which are extensions of the side armour plates.

Marder III Ausf M – again these are late production vehicles. Initially the driving compartment had a cast cover but at the end of 1943 a simpler welded one replaced this.

A highly camouflaged Marder III Ausf M photographed in Normandy. All that can been seen are the driver's compartment and the gun muzzle.

Marder III Ausf M belonging to the 2nd SS Panzer Division caught in the Roncey pocket southeast of Coutances, Normandy, by the American Army in late July 1944.

A Marder III Ausf M amidst the debris in Normandy. This one has the cast cover for the driving compartment, identifying it as an early production vehicle. The object to the left is the remains of a 4x4 amphibious Schwimmwagen.

Chapter Eight

Jagdpanzer 38(t) Hetzer

By March 1943 it was very apparent that the open fighting compartment on the various Panzerjäger based on the highly reliable 38(t) tank left the crew too vulnerable to both direct and indirect enemy fire. Guderian called for a light tank destroyer with a lower profile, better armour and – crucially – overhead protection. This eventually led to the design of the Jagdpanzer 38(t) Hetzer für 7.5cm PaK39 which featured a wide hull and angled armour. Guderian recalled,

> On 7 December [1943] it was decided that the full production capacity of the old Czech 38-ton tank be switched to tank destroyers; these, to be built on Czech tank chassis, and protected by sloping armour plate, were to mount a recoilless gun and a machine-gun with a curved barrel. They passed their tests very satisfactorily. This tank destroyer was intended to be the basic weapon for the anti-tank battalions of the infantry divisions, and thus the belated answer to my proposals made on March the 9th.

Guderian can only have fumed that nine long months had been wasted while a series of unsatisfactory stopgaps had been rushed to the troops at the front instead of an adequately armoured light tank destroyer. The Hetzer was a completely new and dedicated design employing the 38(t) chassis to create an armoured vehicle that was unlike any of its predecessors.

The Hetzer included a much wider hull that took the angled superstructure armour over the top of the tracks and the nose plates forward of the drive sprockets. This made it over a metre longer than the Marder III Ausf M and almost half a metre wider. It had a slightly lower profile and, most importantly, an armoured roof. It was more than 5 tons heavier than the Marder III, and to take the extra weight the eight rubber-tyred road wheels were slightly larger. The single central return roller used on the Marder III Ausf M was also retained.

The frontal armour on the superstructure, gun mantlet and hull was 60mm, while the sides were protected by 20mm. This was a vast improvement on its predecessors but not on the StuG and Jagdpanzer, which enjoyed up to 80mm of armour. However, the Hetzer's armour was much enhanced by its 60 degree angle on the front and 40 degree angle on the sides. This meant that it enjoyed the equivalent protection of 120mm of armour on the front. The vehicle also featured a roof-mounted remote control machine gun to provide close protection. Essentially the infantry had been provided with a much-needed miniature version of the Jagdpanther.*

Initially the decision to proceed with the vehicle was on the basis that it would have a novel fixed non-recoiling mount for the 75mm PaK39 gun. It was known as the Jagdpanzer 38(t) Starr (meaning inflexible – referring to the gun mounting). The plan was that it would speed up production, while the recoil would simply be passed through the hull and chassis, although this innovation would undoubtedly not have added to crew comfort. The practicalities of implementing the design proved a headache, however, and just ten pre-production Starrs were ever built. The installation of the troubled rigid mounting for the PaK39 and the StuH42 was progressively deferred and was eventually overtaken by the end of the war.

In the event the Hetzer went into production with a recoiling gun, and nine of the pre-production Starrs were converted into Hetzers. To overcome the space limitations, the 75mm PaK39 L/48 gun was installed in a compact mounting and offset to the right. This greatly restricted the traverse, permitting just 5 degrees to the left and 11 degrees to the right. It also made the vehicle nose-heavy and put extra weight on the right-hand suspension. The PaK39 was not fitted with a muzzle brake but fired a solid 6.8kg projectile that could cut through 82mm of armour at 1,000m. For close-in defence the Hetzer relied on the vulnerable roof-mounted remote control machine gun.

BMM commenced production of the Hetzer and Skoda also took it up in July 1944. From April 1944 until the end of the war in May 1945 some 2,584 Hetzers rolled off the production line in Prague. In light of Nazi Germany's failing fortunes this was a quite an achievement. Output was to be ramped up in 1945 with a thousand Hetzers every month by mid-year. The compact Hetzer proved ideal for Germany's defensive battles, but the limited traverse on the 75mm gun and the extremely cramped fighting compartment were major drawbacks for the four-man crew.

There were three non-anti-tank Hetzer variants but these were never built in any great quantity. To support the Hetzer units in the field about 170 Bergepanzer 38(t) Hetzer armoured recovery vehicles were constructed. Production in the summer of 1944 was so slow that sixty-four regular Hetzers were converted to the recovery role. Dedicated production was then resumed at the end of the year. The Bergepanzer 38(t) had no gun, a lower superstructure and was open-topped. A tubular crane derrick and a winch were carried in the open fighting compartment.

---

* The Jagdpanzer is covered in Anthony Tucker-Jones, *The Panther Tank: Hitler's T-34 Killer* (Pen & Sword, 2016)

These recovery vehicles were underpowered and therefore struggled in their allotted role.

Two combat variants of the Hetzer were produced at the end of 1944. One consisted of just thirty self-propelled heavy infantry guns known as the 150mm Schweres Infanteriegeschütz 33/2 (sf) au Jagdpanzer 38(t) Hetzer. This used the Bergepanzer 38(t) superstructure, which was raised around the SiG33 150mm gun. These were employed to supplement the existing Grille 38(t) self-propelled guns.

To support the Ardennes Offensive twenty Flammpanzer 38(t) flamethrowers were hastily converted from existing Hetzers. The 75mm gun was replaced with a 14mm Flammenwerfer 41 that had a range of up to 60m. Some 700 litres of flame fuel was carried internally and provided 87.5 seconds of fire. From a distance the Flammpanzer looked like a regular Hetzer as a dummy funnel-shaped barrel was installed over the flamethrower.

During the Ardennes Offensive Flammpanzer 38(t) served with the 352nd and 353rd Panzer Flamm Companies attached to Army Group G. Most of them subsequently ended up with the 13th SS Corps and were lost in the fighting for the Lower Vosges mountains.

As noted, the Jagdpanzer 38(t) was not used to equip the panzer battalions, but instead was deployed with the infantry divisions' Sturmgeschütz companies that had not been equipped with the ubiquitous StuG assault gun. It served on the Eastern Front and in the West, particularly during the Ardennes Offensive. The first combat units equipped with the Hetzer were Panzerjäger Battalions 731 and 743, along with the 15th and 76th Infantry Divisions. After that they were widely distributed. The Hetzer first entered service in the Waffen-SS with the assault gun battalion of the 8th SS Kavallerie Division Florian Geyer, though the deployment of this tank destroyer did little to save the division. It was annihilated in Budapest in February 1945 by the Red Army, along with its sister division, the 22nd Freiwilligen Kavallerie Division der SS Maria Theresia.

In February 1945, just three months before the end of the war, plans were drawn up for a Panzerjäger 38(d) series. This was to have provided a short-term light tank replacement until the E-10 was ready, with tank destroyer, anti-aircraft, reconnaissance, armoured personnel and armoured weapons carrier variants. Development of a self-propelled version armed with a 75mm gun was given priority in 1944–45, presumably as a replacement for the Hetzer. The Germans were planning to turn production of the Panzerjäger 38(d) over to the German factories that had produced the Panzer III and IV. The aim was to produce 2,000 a month but with the end of the war the project was abandoned.

The Czech-built chassis was deemed so successful that the Germans were planning to continue using it once they had won the war! Plans had been afoot for a new 10.5-ton light reconnaissance tank dubbed the T-15 and a 22-ton medium tank known as the T-25. Both were to use a lengthened and widened version of the Skoda 38(t) chassis with sloping armour, thought to have been influenced by the T-34. In light of Germany's crumbling defences neither tank got much beyond the design stage. In late 1944 and early 1945 the Wehrmacht was also planning a tracked troop carrier using a stretched 38(t) chassis, but this project was abandoned as well. Once the Red Army had captured Prague, production of the Hetzer came to a halt.

One new successor Czech vehicle that almost got off the ground was the Waffentrager self-propelled gun that was to use 38(t) components. Development of this gun carriage with two variants began in 1943 with armament ranging from an 88mm gun to a 150mm howitzer. The drawings for both were ready by March 1945 and moves toward production were being made. It was intended that this would commence in the spring of 1945 with an output of up to 350 vehicles a month. Components were to come from both the 38(t) and 38(d) programmes and once again production would have been turned over to German firms such as Ardelt in Eberswalde.

The Hetzer, based on the ubiquitous Czech-designed PzKpfw 38(t) light tank, amounted to a miniature version of the Jagdpanther. They left the Czech factories in dunkel gelb (deep sand yellow) overpainted with distinctive large lobed patterns using olivgrun (olive green) and rotbraun (reddish brown). The initial production Hetzer was nose-heavy and some required modification.

Hitler inspecting a Panzerjäger unit issued with Hetzers fresh from the factory. The vehicles have the basic factory finish of dunkel gelb. The crews are dressed in black panzertruppen-style uniforms rather than Sturmartillerie field-grey.

Captured at Halloville in northeastern France in late 1944 by the American Army, this Hetzer has been painted in the German 'ambush scheme'. This consisted of large spots of olivgrun and rotbraun over dunkel gelb, with the large spots stippled all over with small spots in the first two colours. This replicated the shadows created by sunlight through foliage and made the vehicles almost impossible to detect when they were also camouflaged with branches. At least two rounds have penetrated the right-hand side armour of this vehicle. The gun mantlet is the later lighter version.

A well camouflaged Hetzer lies abandoned at the roadside; one of the dead crew can be seen just to the right. This shot shows how the Pak39 75mm gun was offset to the right.

This photograph gives a very clear indication of how well armoured the gun mounting was behind the Saukopfblende. The 75mm gun could only traverse 5 degrees to the left and 11 degrees to the right; in contrast the Marder could manage about 25 degrees in either direction.

Two captured Hetzers. The crew of the vehicle on the right stored their helmets on the outside of the vehicle, probably because the low angled armour inevitably meant that the fighting compartment was very cramped.

Three more captured Hetzers in fairly pristine condition at a vehicle dump awaiting disposal. The rear of the vehicle on the right has one of several exhaust layout variations. As the engine ran hot, the exhaust was kept as short as possible and covered with a muffler and flame-damper.

The dumped Hetzer in the foreground has shed its tracks, while behind it is a Bergepanzer 38(t) Hetzer recovery vehicle. BMM converted sixty-four Hetzers to this role and built another 106 from scratch. This vehicle had a lower superstructure and was open-topped. In the background several Marder are just visible among the debris.

These knocked-out Hetzers have two different finishes. The one on the left has had a winter coat of whitewash, while the one on the right is an indistinct dark colour.

In well concealed ambush positions, the Hetzer proved a deadly menace to Allied tank crews. It was small and easy to conceal, and the front, thanks to the angled armour, had the equivalent of 120mm protection. This vehicle has the initial half cone-shaped outer mantlet, which was replaced in August 1944 by a lighter and more conical-looking mantlet.

A Hezter keeping company with a Panther tank. The Hetzer has been described as a mini Jagdpanther. This particular vehicle also has the earlier half-cone mantlet.

Photographed in the closing stages of the war, both the Hetzers nearest the camera have lost road wheels.

A Hetzer knocked out on the streets. Its compact profile made it ideal for urban warfare. Six different styles of idler wheel were used, which had varying numbers of holes.

Captured at the Skoda factory at Pilsen in Czechoslovakia in 1945, it is unlikely that this late production model Hetzer saw any combat. However, this vehicle has clearly not just come off the production line, so it is equally possible it had been returned to the factory for refurbishment. Skoda maintained production right up until the end of the war.

This is a very rare example of the *Jagdpanzer* 38(t) Starr that never went into production. It featured a non-recoiling gun mount, which in theory should have made it easy to produce. Note the much smaller and narrower gun mantlet. However, as a result of manufacturing difficulties, it was swiftly superseded by the Hetzer design.

The rear of the Starr has a square rather than round plate giving access to the transmission. The exhaust layout is also different from other models.

Chapter Nine

Panzer or Assault Gun?

While the Western Allies dabbled with the tank destroyer concept utilising the Sherman tank, it was the Soviets who were most impressed by the Sturmgeschütz. Employing the T-34 tank chassis, the Soviets produced the SU-122 (actually a self-propelled howitzer rather than a true anti-tank weapon), the SU-85 and the SU-100 tank destroyers,* followed by the ISU-122 and ISU-152 on the modified KV tank chassis. For the assault gun role the Soviets created the SU-76, which married a 76.2mm gun to the chassis of the T-70 light tank. Production of this compact self-propelled gun was only surpassed by the T-34.

The German assault gun requirement arose from a need to provide the infantry with an armoured vehicle that could serve as both a mobile artillery support weapon and an anti-tank gun. Increasingly the tank destroyer role took over, especially on the Eastern Front where the German Army had to contend with ever-growing numbers of Soviet tanks. On the whole the main task of the StuG was to arm the Sturmgeschütz brigades. Not surprisingly, most of these were deployed on the Eastern Front. Between 1942 and 1945 there were up to thirty independent assault gun units fighting the Red Army in what became a war of attrition.

In the summer of 1944 Army Group Centre's armoured forces on the Eastern Front included eight independent Sturmgeschütz brigades that had recently been upgraded from battalion strength. These were spread out through the component armies. The 3rd Panzer Army had two assault gun formations: Sturmgeschütz Brigades 28 and 245 assigned to the 6th and 9th Corps respectively. The 4th Army also had two assault gun brigades, 185 deployed with the 39th Corps and 190 Light Brigade. Under the 2nd Army's direction were Sturmgeschütz Brigades 237 and 904 serving with the 8th Corps.

Army Group Centre lay directly in the path of Stalin's Operation Bagration – the Soviet version of D-Day. It was entirely a defensive formation created largely from infantry divisions; although it included a panzer army and two panzer corps, it had no whole panzer divisions so crucially it lacked tanks. The Panzerjäger battalions of the infantry divisions were armed with self-propelled anti-tank guns, all of which were designed for defensive rather than offensive operations.

---

* See Anthony Tucker-Jones, *T-34: The Red Army's Legendary Medium Tank* (Pen & Sword, 2015)

Army Group Centre mustered just three panzergrenadier divisions and their panzer battalions were equipped with assault guns, not tanks. A typical panzergrenadier division consisted of two panzergrenadier regiments, a tank battalion with three batteries of StuGs and a Panzerjäger battalion with three companies of self-propelled anti-tank guns and a company of self-propelled anti-aircraft or flak guns. A StuG battery numbered up to fourteen vehicles. An artillery regiment with about four batteries of guns provided fire support.

The 18th Panzergrenadier Division's principal units consisted of Panzergrenadier Regiments 30 and 51, Panzer Abteilung 118 equipped with Sturmgeschütz, Panzerjäger Abteilung 118 equipped with self-propelled anti-tank guns and Artillery Regiment 18. Likewise the 25th Panzergrenadier Division consisted of Panzer Abteilung 8, Panzerjäger Abteilung 125, Artillery Regiment 25 and Panzergrenadier Regiments 35 and 119. Panzergrenadier Division Feldherrnhalle had a similar organisation; it had started out as the 60th Motorised Infantry Division, but under Generalmajor Hans-Adolf von Arenstorff had been largely destroyed during the fighting for Stalingrad.

The veteran 20th Panzer Division was reassigned to Army Group Centre in mid-June 1944 with just a single battalion of panzers. The division comprised a weak panzer regiment, two panzergrenadier regiments, an artillery regiment and a Panzerjäger battalion armed with self-propelled guns. At best it could muster two Kampfgruppen or battle groups organised around the armoured and infantry formations. As a fighting reserve it was wholly inadequate and could only respond to a single breakthrough or would be fatally weakened by being committed piecemeal to various sectors. When the time came, Army Group Centre's StuGs and Panzerjäger were unable to stop the Red Army breaking through en masse.

In Normandy the StuG equipped many of the tank destroyer battalions of the panzer divisions. This was the case with the 1st and 2nd SS Panzer Divisions. All the other divisions (apart from the 9th and 10th SS which did not have tank destroyer battalions in Normandy) employed the StuG to bolster their obsolete Marder and limited numbers of Jagdpanzer IV. When the battle for Normandy commenced, the StuG III and the rarer StuG IV were standing in for the Panzer IV in two companies of the 2nd SS, 9th SS and 10th SS Panzer Divisions. These units were mainly equipped with the StuG III Ausf G.

In the case of the 17th SS Panzergrenadier Division its panzer battalion was equipped with forty-two StuG III, while the Panzerjäger battalion had a dozen Marder self-propelled guns. Initially the independent Sturmgeschütz Battalion 902 with another thirty-one StuG III was assigned to the 17th SS, but it ended up in southern France with the German 19th Army. Confusingly, the numbers for Panzergruppe West, controlling German armour in Normandy, included tanks, assault guns and tank destroyers, but not light tanks, self-propelled guns or armoured cars.

In Normandy the German infantry divisions' anti-tank battalions largely consisted of towed weapons, but at least six army Panzerjäger battalions were also each equipped with fourteen Marder self-propelled and ten Sturmgeschütz assault guns (these served with the 243rd, 326th 331st, 346th, 352nd and 353rd Infantry Divisions).

The battle for Normandy also involved three independent StuG brigades (12, 341, 394) and two independent StuG battalions (902 and 1348). These units were not very strong and only fielded a total of 148 assault guns between them. There were also three independent Panzerjäger battalions but one of them only had towed guns. Of the remaining two, one (654) was a heavy tank hunter battalion equipped with limited numbers of Jagdpanther.

The Jagdpanzer IV developed to replace the StuG only began to enter service at the beginning of 1944 and was in the process of replacing the Marder in the tank destroyer battalions. They were rare in Normandy, with only about sixty available, spread across five panzer divisions; on average each battalion had about a dozen.

In the South of France Army Group G lost all its armoured units (with the exception of the 11th Panzer Division), including Sturmgeschütz Brigade 341. This unit started as a battalion in December 1943, but was reorganised to brigade strength the following February. By May 1944 it was deployed in southern France near Narbonne. By June it had nineteen StuG III and nine Sturmhaubitze 42s. It remained in southern France for the rest of that month and much of July, having been issued a total of thirty-three StuG IIIs and twelve StuH42s. It was despatched to Normandy on 25 July 1944 and was first committed to combat in the Brécey-Avranches area six days later. By the end of August it had been reduced to just twelve assault guns.

The other independent assault gun units in Normandy did not fare well. For example, Fallschirm Sturmgeschütz Brigade 12 was still forming and undergoing training at the time of D-Day. It appears that it never received its full authorised strength of thirty-one assault guns. By late June 1944 it had just eleven combat-ready StuGs and by the end of July could muster only seven StuG IIIs and three StuH42s. It is unclear how many of these escaped over the Seine. Brigade 394 had thirty-one StuG IIIs by early August but after seeing combat in the Vire area only managed to save a single StuG from the Falaise pocket.

Sturmgeschütz Battalion 902 was fighting in support of the 91st Infantry Division in the Cotentin Peninsula in June 1944 with twenty-one combat-ready StuG IIIs. It escaped encirclement but by early August only had one StuG III and three StuH42s available. In September it was reassigned to 19th Army with ten assault guns. Sturmgeschütz Battalion 1348 went into action with just five assault guns, and another five due for delivery. It arrived in Normandy on 6 August 1944 but nothing further is known about its performance.

After Normandy, assault guns were involved in Hitler's Ardennes Offensive in the winter of 1944/5. While his forces included two whole panzer armies, the German 7th Army lacked armour except for the 5th Parachute Division's Sturmgeschütz Brigade 11 and the panzer units of the 15th Panzergrenadier Division. Two Normandy veterans that took part in the Ardennes Offensive were StuG Brigades 341 and 394 assigned to the 15th Army's 81st and 74th Army Corps respectively. StuG Brigade 394 was reassigned to the 5th Panzer Army's 49th Panzer Corps in the New Year.

Assault guns provided the backbone of the German armoured forces in Italy during the period 1943–45. German panzer divisions were always thin on the ground as they were needed elsewhere. Once the Allies had broken out of their various bridgeheads, the low-profile assault gun proved to be an ideal weapon for the Germans' defensive war in the mountains of Italy. On the whole the German infantry divisions relied on the support of panzergrenadier units, which had fewer armoured fighting vehicles than the regular panzer divisions.

Five panzergrenadier divisions – the 3rd, 15th, 16th SS, 29th and 90th – saw long-term action in Italy. The 15th Panzer Division, having been lost in Tunisia, was reconstituted in Sicily as the 15th Panzergrenadiers and served there and on the mainland. Most of these units started life as motorised infantry divisions and were converted in 1943. On the whole they were equipped with assault guns, not panzers, although the Parachute Panzer Regiment Hermann Göring included a panzer and assault gun battalion. Jagdpanzer IV were issued to the tank hunter detachments of the panzer divisions from March 1944. They first went into action in Italy with the Hermann Göring Division.

Like the panzertruppen, the Sturmartillerie crews produced a number of aces, such as Oberwachtmeister Richard Schramm of Sturmgeschütz Brigade 202. He was awarded the Knight's Cross in December 1942 for destroying forty-four Soviet armoured fighting vehicles. He was later posted missing presumed dead. Schramm's assault gun was nicknamed Sea Devil by its crew. In March 1943, when Guderian requested the 'subordination of all assault artillery to the Inspector General', it was opposed, he recalled, on the grounds that 'the assault artillery was the only weapon which nowadays enabled gunners to win the Knight's Cross'.

Platoon leader Leutnant Walther Oberloskamp with Sturmgeschütz Brigade 667 earned the Knight's Cross on 10 May 1943 after scoring forty kills. The Waffen-SS also produced a number of StuG aces. SS-Sturmbannführer Walter Kniep commanded the 2nd StuG Battalion of the 2nd SS Panzer Division, which from 5 July 1943 to 17 January 1944 claimed a total of 129 Soviet tanks. Kniep was also awarded the Knight's Cross.

Sturmartillerie crews had their own battle badges. The Allgemeines Sturmabzeichen (General Assault Badge) was instigated in June 1940 and was frequently awarded to self-propelled artillery and anti-tank units. Specifically, it was awarded to personnel involved in three attacks on three different days but who did not qualify for the Infantry Assault or Panzer Battle (Panzerkampfabzeichen) badges – i.e., artillery, anti-tank, anti-aircraft and engineer personnel.

The General Assault Badge was a silver oval made in both cast and stamped versions and was very similar in appearance to the Panzer Assault Badge. It was edged by an oak wreath surrounding a crossed bayonet and stick grenade (rather than a panzer), topped by the folded wing eagle and swastika.

After June 1943, along with the Panzer Battle Badge the General Assault Badge was divided into higher grades, with grades two and three signifying the number of attacks. These had '25' or '50' cartouches at the bottom of the badge wreath; larger, black eagles; and emblems on silver wreaths. The grade four equated to '75', and '100' was larger still, both with gold wreaths. Other awards were worn in the same manner as those awarded to panzer crews: the Knight's Cross was worn at the throat, the Iron Cross 1st Class was pinned to the chest on the left, and the ribbon of the Iron Cross 2nd Class was worn either in the button hole or on a ribbon bar on the left breast.

Regardless of Heinz Guderian's reservations about the development of the Sturmgeschütz and Panzerjäger, they played a major role in the armoured battles fought by Hitler's Wehrmacht. His perceptions were clouded by inter-service rivalry and the fact that 90 per cent of the assault guns were initially outside his terms of reference due to an undoubtedly deliberate clerical error. None the less, Guderian also appreciated that the infantry should be provided with their own dedicated mobile anti-tank weapons and not have to rely on the panzers to fend off enemy tanks.

The lack of mobility with the infantry's towed anti-tank guns and the inadequacy of the initial top-heavy self-propelled anti-tank guns were only ever partially overcome by the StuG and Jagdpanzer. By the time the Hetzer appeared, the tide had already turned against Nazi Germany. In addition, Guderian favoured the panzers because he did not want to face the reality that strategically the Panzerwaffe had gone from being a highly decisive offensive arm to a defensive one. In Italy, France and on the Eastern Front the assault gun constituted a major proportion of Hitler's armoured forces.

The Sturmartillerie crews considered themselves the elite of the artillery and by 1944 claimed to have knocked out 20,000 enemy tanks. The surviving number of StuGs by the end of the war showed that they had borne the brunt of the fighting as much as Guderian's panzers. On 10 April 1945 just 1,053 StuG IIIs and 277 StuH 42s were listed as operational.

A captured StuG III Ausf G redeployed by its new owners. Some StuG were coated not only with Zimmerit anti-magnetic paste, but also with a layer of concrete up to 15cm deep added to the armoured roof of the driving compartment, as seen here.

A Sturmartillerie soldier poses with his StuG III Ausf G. This vehicle has the Saukopfblende gun mantlet and Schürzen fitted, and has been painted in the 1944 stipple effect ambush pattern camouflage. Note the muzzle brake cover.

Abandoned StuG III Ausf G in Noville, Belgium, in 1944. The superstructure has been up-armoured with spare tracks. The wrecked remains of an M4 Sherman and M3 half-track are also visible.

A StuG III Ausf G with Saukopfblende but no Zimmerit or Schürzen (although the rail to hold the side skirts is attached to the superstructure).

These StuG III Ausf G were photographed on the Eastern Front and have a two-tone camouflage in dunkel gelb and rotbraun. Both vehicles are fitted with the Schürzen side skirts to give added protection to the hull and superstructure. These skirts were easily damaged and drivers had a habit of knocking them off. Neither is coated in Zimmerit, which was discontinued towards the end of 1944. The presence of the muzzle covers indicates that the crews were not expecting immediate trouble.

StuG III Ausf G belonging
to the Waffen-SS. Although
both are G models, they
lack the commander's
cupola. Again they do not
have the Zimmerit coating.

The gun mantlet on these StuG III Ausf G are covered in tarpaulin, presumably to keep the rain out. Both have the additional bolt-on nose armour that added 30mm to the existing 50mm nose plates.

A well camouflaged StuG III Ausf G on its way to the front in France. The crew are not wearing their helmets, which were too constricting in the tight confines of the fighting compartment.

Red Army officers examining a StuG III Ausf G. There is no immediate sign of damage so it may have been abandoned after running out of fuel or because of mechanical problems.

A knocked-out StuG III Ausf G in Normandy. The central return roller is missing.

StuG III Ausf G destroyed in the closing months of the war. The first vehicle has lost its forward return roller and has a damaged drive sprocket. Production of the StuG III and IV, as well as the Panzer IV/70, finally ground to a halt in March 1945, while production of the diminutive Hetzer struggled on until the very end of the war in May 1945.

Another StuG III Ausf G destroyed in Normandy. The superstructure has been knocked off the hull.